# CHINESE ART

# CHINESE ART

### Finlay MacKenzie

**PAUL HAMLYN · LONDON**

# ACKNOWLEDGEMENTS

The pieces and paintings in this volume are reproduced by kind permission of the following collections and galleries to which they belong: the British Museum, London (Plates I—III, VI—VIII, X, XIV—XVI, XVIII—XXII, XXIV—XXIX, XXXIV—XXXVI, XL, XLI, XLIV, XLVI, XLVIII); the Victoria and Albert Museum, London (Plates IV, V, IX, XI—XIII); the Percival David Foundation, London (Plates XXX—XXXIII); the Museum of Eastern Art, Oxford (Plate XXIII); the Smithsonian Institution, Freer Gallery of Art, Washington, D. C. (Plates XVII, XXXIX); the Nelson Gallery, Atkins Museum, Kansas City, Missouri (Plate XXXVIII); the Cleveland Museum of Art, Gift of Hanna Fund (Plate XXXVII); the National Gallery of Canada, Ottawa (Plate XLII); Ostasiatiska Museet, Stockholm (Plate XLIII); the Museum für Ostasiatische Kunst, Cologne (Plate XLV); the Author's Collection (Plate XLVII).

The frontispiece is a fragment of an essay by Su Shih, reproduced by permission of the Trustees of the British Museum, London.

First Edition 1961

Second Impression 1963

*Published by*

# PAUL HAMLYN

Westbook House • Fulham Broadway • London

© Paul Hamlyn Ltd 1961

*Printed in Czechoslovakia*

T 1106

# Contents

## Illustrations in the Text

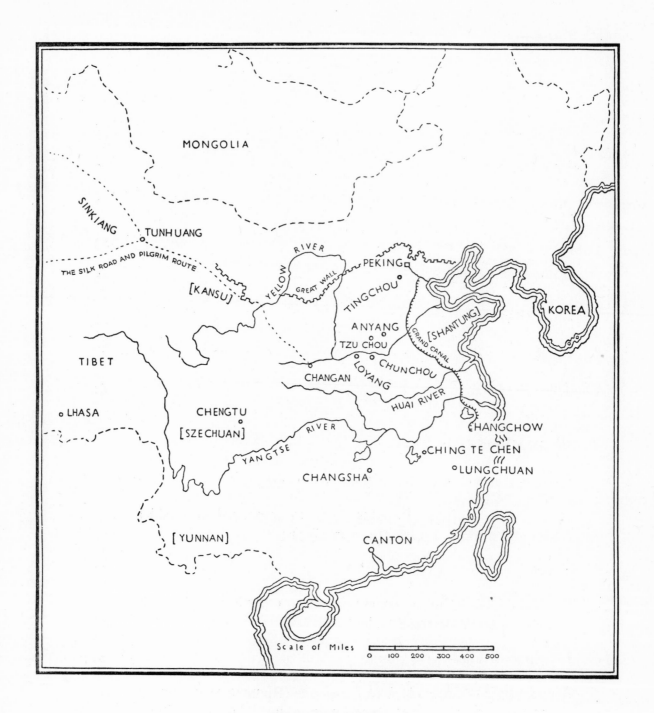

**MAP OF CHINA**

*Names of modern provinces in brackets*

# Introduction

THE civilised world had its beginnings in the valleys of four great rivers: the Nile, the Tigris-Euphrates, the Indus and the Yellow River. The civilisations which grew up in the first three of these each ran their course and then withered and died, and they are known to us only through the tombs and monuments of a long dead past. Chinese civilisation was a late starter (the city of Jericho is some two to three thousand years older than the earliest Chinese city yet discovered), but once it did get started it outlasted all the rest, and the civilisation which is China today is built squarely on the foundations which were laid down some four thousand years ago. It is the oldest living civilisation in the world.

The proto-Chinese tribes who lived in the Yellow River valley some four thousand years ago had settled down in villages of beehive-shaped huts half sunk in the ground for warmth. They supplemented their hunting and fishing by growing millet and keeping pigs. The loess soil was marvellously fertile when watered and could be worked with primitive tools of wood or stone. The chief danger came from the unpredictable flooding of the great river. They had no knowledge of metal or of the wheel in any form, but they were skilled potters and the decorated pots (Plate XVI) which they used for holding grain and for burial with their dead show that they already possessed a discriminating eye for form and texture and surface decoration.

This Neolithic period lasted for some two or three thousand years in China, and Neolithic sites have been discovered spread very widely throughout the central and lower Yellow River basin, north into Manchuria and west into the loess highlands of Kansu. There is little evidence of warfare and there are indications of very far-ranging communications, for they shared their design motifs with other Neolithic peoples spread all across the Eurasian land mass, and they possessed cowrie shells which had come from some far-distant southern seashore.

Some time about 1700 B.C. (the exact date is still in dispute) the armies of Shang

7

burst over the horizons of this peaceful Neolithic world. The great lords rode in clanking horse-drawn chariots, armed and armoured with bronze. The warriors were equipped with bronze dagger-axes, battle axes and spears (Plate I) and with the powerful compound bow reinforced with horn. To the simple Stone Age tribesmen, armed at best with stone axes and hoes, it must have seemed like the end of the world. In fact it was the beginning of civilisation.

Who the Shang were, and where their elaborate Bronze Age culture began and grew to maturity we do not yet know. The earliest evidence yet discovered shows them to be a group of bronze owning aristocrats living off the agricultural labours of their serfs and slaves. They possessed horses and cattle and sheep, and perhaps even domesticated elephants, for one of their written characters distinctly shows a man leading an elephant, and elephants are known to have existed in north China at that time. They could weave silk and other textiles and could produce high-fired wheeled pottery. Their elaborate written language contained over a thousand different characters, while their bronze weapons and sacrificial vessels were the finest that the world has known They lived in fine timbered palaces, and they spent their time in hunting, warfare and elaborate ceremonial.

Some scholars have suggested that they were invading conquerors from the West. This 'Dispersal Theory' claiming that all Eastern civilisation had to be brought from some mysterious font of wisdom in the West was very popular in nineteenth-century Europe, but it has now been discredited. Their skeletal remains show that the Shang were not racially different from the Neolithic tribespeople whom they conquered and enslaved. Their superiority lay in their technology and social organisation, not in their genes. It is probable that they developed out of the Neolithic culture of north-east China. Some finds made in Shantung Province, at a place called Ch'eng Tzu Yai, show the existence of a culture quite different from that of the north-west; the pottery here was black and was turned on the wheel, and the remains of a walled town were found. It is quite possible that further excavations in this area will tell us how and when the culture of Shang grew out of Stone Age barbarism.

For some five centuries the Shang aristocrats lived in their tiny city-states surrounded by their fields and pastures, and then in the eleventh century B.C. they were overthrown by their former vassals, the Chou. The name of the dynasty changed, but the economic and cultural foundations did not. Under the Chou, Chinese city-states began to appear as far afield as the Yangtze valley in the south and in what is now Szechuan Province on the upper Yangtze valley and even in the jungles of Yunnan in the far south-west.

8

This vast geographical spread brought about a weakening of central control, and after 771 B.C. the empire of the Chou broke up into dozens of independent kingdoms. The rulers of these kingdoms were small groups of hereditary lords and warriors whose lives were goverened by tradition and the unchanging feudal code of conduct. But while the social structure remained unchanged, tremendous changes were taking place in the economic and technological fields in the years 771—221 B.C. Cast iron hoes and ploughshares were replacing the old stone hoes and wooden digging sticks, making farming far more productive. Irrigation and flood control had reached such a high level that entire river basins could be controlled and developed as in the case of the Chengkuo canal where a tributary of the Yellow River was harnessed to irrigate over half a million acres. Vast tracts of forest and grassland were opened up to agriculture, communications were improved, metal coinage came into general use and the manufacture of silk, salt and iron was carried out on a large scale with workshops employing several hundred workers.

All these innovations could only be properly developed by large-scale social organisation with unified central authority. The hereditary aristocrats with their vested interest in their small-scale feudal authority, their endless squabblings among themselves, and their concern for the fixed and unchanging feudal code of conduct and of ceremonial were neither willing nor able to make use of them. But in states such as Ch'in on the frontiers of this feudal world, where the old order was not so firmly established, the king was able to carry out sweeping social reforms and establish a unified central control. The new techniques in agriculture and water-control brought in greatly increased revenue which could pay for a more powerful army. This in turn led to territorial conquests and more resources to exploit. The process, of course, was anything but straightforward, and some five centuries of warfare and political struggle had to pass before the state of Ch'in had swallowed up all its rivals and established the unified Chinese empire. The empire of Ch'in was geared for total war and could not cope with the problems of peaceful administration. Within a dozen years it had collapsed and the empire had been taken over by the new dynasty of Han, which was to last for some four hundred years (206 B.C. — 220 A.D.).

The empire of Han stretched south to the jungles of Indo-China, north to the grasslands and deserts, and west to the mountains of Tibet. The unification of the country, the establishment of peace and security after centuries of warfare, the elimination of the feudal aristocracy, the introduction of a money economy so that not only grain and other commodities but even land could be bought and sold, all these factors led to tremendous expansion and the appearance of a vast new class of urban

9

officials and bureaucrats, merchants industrialists and moneyed landowners.

The outlook on life of this new class was quite different from that of the former slave-owning aristocracy. Instead of a fierce pride in noble lineage and a concern with warfare and ceremonial there was a typical *petit bourgeois* concern with material possessions and the comforts of life. As Willets says, 'The inventory of chattels found in their graves reads like the catalogue of a departmental store: lacquered occasional tables with dishes, trays, bowls, spoons and ladles; hats, leather shoes; fragments of silks and woollen clothes, and chests for clothes, seals of office and writing brushes, belt hooks, jewellery, combs, hairpins and mirrors; cosmetic outfits comprising nests of lacquered boxes holding pomades, face powder, powder brushes, rouge and mascara, even a divination set for fortune telling. A civilised self-conscious period evidently. Yet despite its grandeur, perhaps a trifle dull.'* Perhaps, but how much more pleasant than the human heads and immolated dogs and horses and other atrocities found in the Shang tombs of 1500 years before.

One of the greatest achievements of the Han Dynasty was the decisive defeat of the Huns and the opening of the trade routes across the grasslands and deserts of central Asia. This brought China for the first time into contact with the civilisations of western and southern Asia. (The shorter route to India across 'The Hump' into Burma always proved impassable in ancient times. The overland route to India lay right across central Asia, skirting Tibet and the Pamir massif and down into the Indus valley from the north-west.)

It was at this time that the new breed of horses, which figure so largely in Chinese art, were brought to China. The horse indigenous to east Asia is short and stocky, a rather unprepossessing beast. The Emperor Wu (140—86 B.C.), in his war against the Huns, desperately needed good horses to supply his cavalry. One of his envoys to the western regions of central Asia brought back news of the 'Blood Sweating' thoroughbreds of Ferghana which were said to possess miraculous powers of speed and endurance. Ferghana was a remnant of Alexander the Great's empire, and these horses were descended from the Arabian thoroughbreds brought there by his armies some two centuries before. In 106 B.C. the Emperor Wu sent the brother of one of his concubines at the head of an army of several thousand men to capture some of these horses. Only a few survivors reached Ferghana and these were soundly defeated and had to return home empty handed. Chinese prestige was now at stake in central Asia, so in 102 B.C. the Emperor dispatched an army of one hundred thousand men. Only about half of these survived the four thousand mile journey, but Ferghana was

---

* William Willets: *Chinese Art*, p. 175, Penguin Books, 1958.

10

Chariot with outrider. *Rubbing from an impressed clay tablet found in a tomb in Chengtu. Han Dynasty*

duly attacked and a few dozen of the precious horses were brought back to China. From this time on these horses served as an inspiration to Chinese artists. In the Han Dynasty they were pictured on the clay tomb slabs (see illustration above). In the T'ang they were modelled in pottery (Plates XXII, XXIII) and they inspired some of China's greatest painters such as Han Kan, Chao Meng-fu and Li Lung-mien.

In 184 A.D. the Han Dynasty was shaken to its foundations by a peasant rebellion, and although this was put down, real power had slipped into the hands of the generals who now set themselves up as independent war lords. China slid into a dark age of disunion and chaos where she suffered from some four hundred years of civil war and barbarian invasion.

This period (220—589) is known as the Six Dynasties, and is in some ways similar to the Dark Ages through which Europe was passing at about the same time. In both cases a vast empire was broken up and overrun by invading hordes of Huns and other nomad tribes. But nevertheless there are vital differences between the two. In Europe the empire of Rome was completely engulfed, and when after almost a thousand years civilisation once again appeared it was something quite different, built on different foundations, and Rome was but a shadow and a memory. In China on the other hand, although the central authority of the Han empire collapsed completely, Chinese civilisation itself did not disappear even in the areas overrun by the barbarians, indeed it was the culture of the barbarians which collapsed and was absorbed into that of the Chinese. The reason for this does not lie in any mystical Wisdom of the East, but in a fundamental difference in the two empires.

In most of Europe the Roman Empire was an administrative and tax-gathering machine patrolled and pacified by the legions. The economies of the conquered territories were left largely undisturbed so long as the natives paid their taxes and did not rebel. The role of the cities was largely parasitical. They were garrison towns and administrative centres, not the focal points for the economy of the area. When the legions withdrew or were defeated these towns were left like undefended islands in a sea of barbarism, and they were soon engulfed.

In China, on the other hand, while the imperial administration was just as much a tax-gathering machine, the empire itself, Chinese civilisation, was built upon an economic foundation, a way of life, fundamentally different from that of the nomad tribes who lived beyond the borders. The intensive methods of agriculture of the Chinese, their advanced technology and their tightly knit social organisation, all these were left behind when the imperial armies withdrew and eventually triumphed over the less efficient and more loosely organised barbarians. In the localities where wholesale massacres had depopulated whole areas, Chinese civilisation did receive a major setback, but in general we can say that when the Sui (589—618) and the T'ang Dynasties (618—907) restored the unified empire they were able to take up the task where the Han had left off some four hundred years before.

During the Six Dynasties period there was a vast movement of population out of the troubled north into the Yangtze valley and the lands of the south which were still enjoying relative peace. For the first time the south ceased to be an outlying province of the empire and became a centre of culture and civilisation in its own right. This development was consolidated in the Sui Dynasty when a series of canals was built culminating in the Grand Canal which linked the Yangtze valley with the Yellow River valley. The great cities on this line of communication reached new heights of prosperity. Ch'ang An in the north-west was the terminus of the great overland routes across central Asia, and was also connected through the Wei and Yellow Rivers to the rest of the country. Loyang, the eastern capital in Sui and T'ang times, was at the juncture of the Yellow River and the Grand Canal. Yangchow, on the spot where the Grand Canal enters the Yangtze, was the hub of the rich trade of the Lower Yangtze valley, and Chengtu on an upper tributary of the Yangtze carried on a thriving trade with the lands of the south-west. The enormous expenditure on public works during the Sui Dynasty caused such hardship among the people that the dynasty was overthrown after only twenty-eight years, but the T'ang Dynasty which followed it in 618 was able to reap the benefit of these labours.

The first one hundred and thirty years of the T'ang Dynasty made up one of the most glorious periods of Chinese history. During this time the dynasty was blessed with three rulers of supreme ability. Li Shih-min, known as the Emperor T'ang Tai Tsung, the real founder of the dynasty, who is often spoken of as the greatest of all Chinese emperors; the Empress Wu who fought her way to the throne with blood-thirsty ruthlessness and yet brought twenty years of peace and prosperity to the empire; and lastly T'ang Ming Huang who brought the empire to the peak of its prosperity and cultural splendour, and then, alas, in the foolishness of his old age saw the whole splendid fabric torn to shreds.

During these hundred and thirty years not only did agriculture prosper, especially in the rice-growing lands of central and southern China, but arts and handicrafts were flourishing. Szechuan Province produced gold and silverwares and fine brocades, while porcelain of the highest quality was made in several centres. Lacquer wares came from Hsiangyang and bronze mirrors from Yangchou; tribute silk for the court came from Tingchou. Chinese merchant vessels as much as 200 feet long sailed to India, Persia, Arabia and the South Sea Islands. Persian and Arab traders brought spices, drugs and gem stones and exchanged them at Canton for porcelain, silk, tea, bronze mirrors and ironware. Traders from central Asia brought carpets, turquoise, jade and furs to the capital.

Ch'ang An, the capital, was the largest and most civilised city in the world of that time. It was, says Obata, 'a great cosmopolitan city where Syrians, Arabs, Persians, Tartars, Tibetans, Koreans, Japanese and Tonkinese and other peoples of widely divergent races and faiths lived side by side, presenting a remarkable contrast to the ferocious religious and racial strife then prevailing in Europe'. The city boasted some two million inhabitants and was carefully laid out according to plan. At the court were gathered some of the greatest poets, artists and scholars in Chinese history: Li Po, Tu Fu, Po Chu-i, and a host of other poets. 'Whoever was a man was a poet,' said one writer of the period, and one anthology of T'ang poetry contains 48,900 poems by 2,200 poets. Wu Tao-tzu and Li Ssu-hsun, two of the greatest names in the history of Chinese painting, were covering the walls of Buddhist temples with their frescoes.

The Emperor Li Shih-min founded a university and a library containing over two hundred thousand volumes. Civil service examinations were founded as a means of choosing the army of officials required to administer the empire, and in the eighth century the Han Lin Academy was founded to act as a centre for the most learned scholars of the day. It was to serve as the model for the academies which were founded in Europe a thousand years later.

Suddenly, in the middle of the eighth century this whole splendid edifice collapsed with dramatic suddenness. In 751 the Arabs attacked the western frontiers, and at the Battle of the Talas River overwhelmed the Chinese garrisons. This was one of the decisive battles of the world, for it destroyed China's power in central Asia and cut her off from the overland trade routes to the west and to India. It also sealed the fate of Buddhism in that area. What had been one of the great strongholds of the faith became in time converted to Islam, and Mohammedanism was to spread far into north-west China and even into Yunnan Province in the south-west.

In China itself, corruption and the monopolisation of land in the hands of the officials was weakening the empire. In 755 the An Shih rebellion broke out, Ch'ang An was sacked, and the north-west was pillaged and plundered to such an extent that it was never again the centre of the empire. The rebellion was eventually put down and the dynasty lasted for another one hundred and fifty years, but the Golden Age was gone.

The ninth and tenth centuries which saw the collapse of the T'ang and the passage of the troubled Five Dynasties was a time of political upheaval and of some vicious dynastic infighting, but apart from the ravaged areas in the north-west, the country at large continued on its way much as before, and the Sung Dynasty which came to power in 960 can be looked on as a continuation of the T'ang. Gone was the almost frenzied energy, the boundless hunger for far horizons and the eagerness for the new and the strange. The host of foreign influences, even Buddhism itself, became absorbed and synthesised into purely Chinese forms. The lyric poetry of the T'ang gave place to the calm philosophic speculation of Chu Hsi and his Neo-Confucianism. In ceramics the striking forms and bold contrasting glazes changed to the elegant subtlety of Sung porcelain. In painting, the sweeping lines and bold colours became the muted tones and introspective landscapes of Ma Yuan, Hsia Kuei and a host of others.

Militarily speaking, the Sung Dynasty was a fiasco. Even at the height of its power it never controlled as large an area as the T'ang, or even the Han Dynasty. It never managed to break through the lines of Tartars which hemmed it in from the north and north-west, and in 1127 the Emperor Hui Tsung managed to get himself and his entire court of over 3,000 people carried off into captivity, never to return. When one of the younger princes managed to re-establish the capital of the dynasty at Hangchou, south of the Yangtze, the military defeats continued, and the patriotic general Yueh Fei, who was carrying out a successful campaign to recover the lost lands of the north, was murdered in 1141 by his political rivals, and his efforts came to nothing.

But this sorry tale should not obscure the enormous achievements of Chinese art, science and industry in this period. International trade continued through the seaports of the south. Cities such as Hangchou, the Kinsai of Marco Polo, were enjoying a degree of sophisticated elegance and comfort which was beyond the wildest dreams of the Europeans of that time (the Hangchou described so wonderingly by Marco Polo in the thirteenth century was not in its prime for it had been attacked and occupied by the Mongols.)

The civil service examination system was by now well established, and this tended to relegate the military men to the inferior position which was to be their lot throughout the following centuries. The struggle for power during the Sung Dynasty was to take place between rival politicians and economists. For many years the reformers, led by the Prime Minister Wang An-shih, were able to carry out very far-reaching reforms. Millions of acres of land were brought under cultivation, more than ten thousand water conservancy projects were completed. Mining of precious metals as well as of iron was carried out on an unprecedented scale. Silk spinning and weaving, porcelain manufacture and the printing of books were all encouraged by the government. Price controls for grain were instituted, together with low interest loans and many other government measures designed to increase the prosperity of the common people (and thus increase the imperial revenues). These reforms naturally aroused the bitter opposition of the more conservative landlords and officials, and after the death of Wang An-shih and his patron the Emperor Shen Tsung in 1085, they were discarded.

Important technical advances were being made at this time which were to have profound effects not only in China but throughout the world. For centuries the compass had been used in a primitive form by necromancers, but in the Sung Dynasty a more practical form was developed for navigation, and this was a powerful stimulus to overseas trade. A less happy invention was that of gunpowder which was to revolutionise the science of warfare. Printing had been known for centuries, but now a practical form of moveable type was invented which made printing very much faster and cheaper. Popular literature became a practical possibility.

When the court moved to Hangchou, the Academy of Painting was established as an independent institution in the Ling Yin Temple, and for the remainder of the dynasty it continued to attract the greatest painters in the land. Perhaps the best known are

Ma Yuan and Hsia Kuei, but there were many others of almost equal stature. During these years the art of painting in China reached heights which it never equalled before or since.

But while China was enjoying this Golden Age, the threat of nomad invasion was taking shape in the north-west. As early as 1206 an obscure Mongol named Temuchin had organised all the tribes of Mongolia under his own banner and had himself appointed Genghis Khan. Five years later he led his combined forces against north China. The victory was neither quick nor easy, and some sixty-five years of bitter warfare were to ensue before the last Chinese resistance collapsed and the Mongols were masters of all of China. Genghis had died and his grandson Kublai Khan mounted the Dragon Throne. For the first time the barbarians controlled the entire empire. This meant far more than a simple dynastic change. The eighty-eight years of the Mongol occupation were a major catastrophe for Chinese civilisation. The population dropped from an estimated one hundred million in 1125 to forty-five million in 1329, and more than seven million of these were officially admitted to be starving. Many hitherto prosperous areas were utterly laid waste and the supervision of agriculture and water control was neglected. But it was more than a question of bloodshed and physical destruction. Something seemed to have broken in the spirit of China's ruling class of landed gentry. Never again could they regain the exuberant self-confidence of the T'ang Dynasty or the mellow serenity of the Sung. In the dynasties which were to follow they were to enjoy periods of prosperity and of imperial expansion, but from this time on, Chinese culture was on the defensive, seeking to preserve the fading glories of the past.

During the Mongol (Yuan) Dynasty the civil service examinations were discontinued and the Academy disbanded. Many scholars, cut off from imperial patronage, turned to the wider public offered by the stage and the printing press. This was the period when drama attained great popularity and playwrights such as Kuan Han-ching became national heroes. A few painters such as Chao Meng-fu were willing to serve at the barbarian court, but the majority, working independently, continued the traditions of the Sung, and for a while at least were able to stem the tide of academic formalism that had already begun to creep over the Academy.

In 1368 the Mongols were finally driven out, and China was once more united under a Chinese dynasty, the Ming (1368—1644). There followed a period of restoration and economic development. With the expansion of trade and commerce a new city working class and middle class were appearing and demanding new forms of art to suit their own tastes. This was the great age of the novel and other popular literature,

16

and of the decorative arts. The 'Porcelain City' of Ching Te-chen in central China became a vast factory town turning out hundreds of tons of porcelain for the entire country and yet retaining enough of the fine artistic traditions of the past to preserve very high standards of quality. The silk industry in east China employed thousands of workers, and in the seventeenth century the city of Nanking alone had 50,000 looms, some factories holding as many as 600 looms. The metalworking and mining industries, tea processing and cotton spinning also employed many thousands of workers. China was going through the beginnings of an industrial revolution. But political power was still in the hands of the land-owning gentry and officials, who were not ready to tolerate any real challenge to their position.

In 1644 the Ming Dynasty was replaced by the Ch'ing or Manchu Dynasty. But the Manchu, unlike their fellow Tartars the Mongols, set themselves out to be more Chinese than the Chinese; to preserve intact the entire fabric of the empire so as to extract its wealth for themselves. This led to a period of blind conservatism in both the economic and cultural fields. The Manchu were terrified that any innovation might upset the delicate balance of power which was so profitable to themselves.

The release from this impasse came from two sources — from the long-suffering peasants and new middle class, and from the unexpected quarter of a new type of 'Foreign Barbarian', armed not only with superior firearms but with more advanced economic weapons which were to destroy the foundations upon which the Chinese empire had rested for two thousand years.

As early as 1514 Portuguese traders and buccaneers had appeared off the southern coast of China. After 1565 the Spaniards, using the Philippines as their base, were distributing Chinese silks, porcelain and other goods to Mexico, Chile and their other American possessions. But the real impact of the West was not felt until the nineteenth century when Britain and the other powers flooded the Chinese market with their manufactured goods. There is no room here to go into the story of the collapse of the Chinese empire in 1911 and the emergence of a re-united China. It is enough to say that the Chinese economy and culture, weakened by almost three hundred years of foreign occupation and blind conservatism, could offer only token resistence to the changes which were taking place. The economic and political structure of the empire had outworn its time.

Whatever form the culture of the new China will take, all indications point to the fact that it will be based firmly on the riches of the old tradition, the culture of the oldest living civilisation of the world.

# Bronzes

THE Bronze Age in China can be said to cover roughly the two dynasties of the Shang and the Chou, that is approximately from the eighteenth to the third century B.C. During this time vast numbers of bronze vessels and weapons were cast (over twelve thousand are known to have survived to our own day), and they gave their name to a whole epoch. But it was a Bronze Age in a sense quite different from that of the Stone Age which preceded it or the Iron Age which followed. Bronze was never the chief material for the tools of production of its time. The tools used by the common people in their farming and handicrafts remained much as they had done for centuries. Bronze was always a rare and costly metal jealously monopolised by the ruling class. As the bronze weapons gave these rulers the physical means of suppressing their slaves and serfs, so the sacred vessels of bronze served as their symbols of status, living proof of their exalted rank and noble lineage.

Many of the weapons which have survived from this period must have been made specially for ceremonial or symbolic use for they are far too delicate and finely wrought to have stood up to the conditions of actual warfare (e.g. the halberd in Plate I). Some are inlaid with silver or turquoise, others are partly made up of jade or other costly materials. Some, such as the battle-axe and spear head in Plate I are obviously real weapons of war, but the form and decoration in each case is appropriate to its grim purpose.

The bronze vessels were used at the solemn ceremonies in which the Shang and Chou aristocrats celebrated some great event such as the granting of a fiefdom by the king, or in which they paid homage to their ancestors. Some vessels served as wine goblets (see the *Chia* [Plate III], the *Chüeh* [Plate II], and *Ku* [Plate IV]), others as vessels for holding wine (see the *Tsun* in Plate V). Still others were cooking vessels to hold the sacrificial food, or pans or ewers for holding water. In size they varied from cups and goblets which could be held in the hand, up to gigantic cauldrons over three

*Three 'T'ao T'ieh' ('Devil Mask')*

and a half feet high and weighing half a ton. The beauty of these vessels consists not only in their general form, but also in their surface decoration which originally, no doubt, was full of religious symbolism, but which even to us, some three thousand years later, is strangely moving. It is made up of a combination of abstract patterns, such as the squared spiral and the 'Interlocking T', with highly stylised animal forms such as dragons, tigers, serpents, cicadas and nameless mythical beasts.

The most common motif is the 'Devil Mask' or 'T'ao T'ieh' which usually consists of two serpents or monsters seen in profile facing each other, their forms combining to make up the full-face mask of a larger beast which might be a tiger but is more likely to be a horned bull or ox. In Plate v the vessel as a whole is shaped like an owl (regarded in China today as a bird of ill-omen), but the wings are made up of a serpent within whose coils there are strange monsters crawling among the spirals of the 'Thunder Pattern'. This tendency to shift and alter before our eyes gives this decoration a dream-like, one might almost say nightmare, quality. For throughout the art of this period there runs an undercurrent of horror and darkness, a subtle blend of savagery and sophistication, and therein lies its peculiar fascination.

The method used in casting almost all these vessels is that known as *cire perdue* or 'Lost Wax'. In this method a wax model is first made which conforms in every detail of form and surface decoration to the projected bronze. On this wax model is brushed a thinly diluted wash of clay which is then allowed to dry. Successive coats of clay are applied until the wax model is completely surrounded by a firm mould of clay. Through this clay mould holes called 'runners' are made, through which the wax can run out. The mould is then put in a furnace which hardens the clay and melts the wax which runs out through the runners. Molten bronze, usually 85 % copper and 15 % tin in these ancient vessels, is poured in through the runners to fill up the space left by the wax. When this is cool the clay mould is broken off, the rods left in the runners are removed, and the cut surfaces are smoothed off. The whole procedure is a delicate and dangerous one, and in casting even the simplest object there is always a danger that an air bubble or some small obstruction will interrupt the flow of the bronze and so cause a flaw. How these ancient craftsmen were able to cast the fantastically elaborate shapes and delicate surfaces of these vessels and achieve results so technically perfect taxes one's imagination.

The chemical reactions caused by burial in the ground for some three thousand years have produced an astonishing variety of surface corrosion. Sometimes this is blue or green, at others it is rust-red or silver (as when the copper has been leached out of the bronze, leaving the tin). Sometimes the surface has roughened into lava-like formations, at others it is the smooth grey-green of old bone. In our eyes this surface corrosion lends an added beauty to the pieces and speaks most eloquently of the enormous reach of time which separates us from the original users. It heightens the dark mystery which surrounds these sacrificial vessels, and softens the grim purposefulness of the weapons.

After the Han Dynasty (206 B.C.—220 A.D.) the casting of bronze vessels was largely discontinued, but by the time of the Sung Dynasty, a thousand years later,

**20**

*Shang Dynasty bronze, c. 1400 B.C. (detail)*

*Northern Wei tomb tablet, c. 400 A.D. (detail)*

*Ming tomb tablet, c. 1400 A.D. (detail)*

*These rubbings show the development from bold stylisation to over-ornamentation, resulting in a weakening of design.*

the emperor and his court were showing a lively antiquarian interest in the Shang and Chou vessels which had been taken from ancient tombs. They not only admired their aesthetic qualities, but regarded them as possessing a certain mystical quality, so that by their very presence they lent something of the weight of their ancient authority to their possessors. This led to some brisk activity among the grave-robbing fraternity who as early as the tenth century had discovered some of the Shang graves at Anyang. Ever since that time vessels have been unearthed and many hundreds of ancient tombs despoiled. Fortunately, in recent years, scientific archaeological excavation has taken the place of indiscriminate looting, and enormously rich sites have been uncovered not only at Anyang, but at Chengchow, Hui Hsien and other localities, and we can hope that within the next few years a body of scientific knowledge will have been built up which will enable us to have a much richer and more complete picture of China's Bronze Age.

In the Ming and Ch'ing Dynasties (that is between 1368 and 1911) many ritual bronzes were cast in an attempt to recapture some of the grandeur of the early dynasties, but these are over-elaborate, weak in both form and surface decoration and not to be compared with the work of high antiquity.

One form of bronze casting which retained its vigour right up until T'ang times (618—907) was the making of small animal figures in the form of buckles or amulets. The leaping tiger in Plate VI and the conventionalised lion (Plate XIV) are good examples of this art. They are wonderfully expressive and the stylisation enhances their power. A related group of bronzes is illustrated in Plate VII. These Ordos bronzes, so called from the stretch of grassland and desert enclosed in the great northward swing of the Yellow River where many of them were found, are part of a great family of similar bronze figures found right across the steppe lands of Asia and Europe, sometimes known as Scythian bronzes. These Scythian bronzes were the work of the nomad tribesmen of the steppe and they possess a vigour and keen sense of linear design which they share with the Chinese metalwork of the first and second millennia B.C. In the case of the Ordos bronzes there was obviously an exchange of influence between the settled lands of China and the steppe. At the moment we cannot know for certain who first influenced whom, but some of the finds from the royal tombs at Anyang which are in this style seem to indicate that it was first developed in China during the second millennium B.C. and from there spread to the steppe peoples.

# Pottery and Porcelain

THE earliest Chinese pottery of which we have any record is the Neolithic ware from the river plains and loess highlands of north and north-west China. It was made between 5000 and 2000 B.C. and consists of bowls, jars, pots and beakers of low-fired earthenware. Most of it is utilitarian ware of dull grey or buff colour of little aesthetic interest. But a proportion of it consists of very much finer ware, buff-coloured with fine textured surface, splendidly modelled shapes with black and red decoration in designs of criss-cross lines and sweeping curves which not only please the eye, but subtly enhance the round swelling fullness of the pottery shape. Some of these have been given the name of Yangshao pottery from the village in Honan Province where they were first discovered, but the finest of them have been found in the loess highlands of Kansu Province (Plate XVI). Both in shape and decoration these pots bear a striking resemblance to others found all across the Eurasian land mass and as far away as the Crimea in the south of Russia, and this indicates that people or at least ideas were free to travel across these enormous distances during Neolithic times.

These pots were not turned on a wheel but were built up by what is known as the Coil Method. That is, a long sausage of clay was wound carefully up into a coil shape and this coil was smoothed and patted by hand into the shape of a pot. The makers were Stone Age barbarians, but they showed the most astonishing sensitivity to form and symmetry. There has been a great deal of speculation about the religious symbolism of the decoration; for instance it has been suggested that the thin red line running between the two jagged lines of black represents the blood of life flowing between the perils of death and destruction. It is very probable that the designs did have some religious significance, but at this distance in time we can only guess at what it was.

Farther east, in the seacoast province of Shantung, there have been found shards of fine wheel-turned black pottery with a smooth polished surface and a thickness in some cases of no more than a millimetre. Very little of this ware has been seen outside of China, but since the shape of the vessels suggests that they were the prototypes of the Shang bronze shapes, it is possible that here we have the intermediate stage between the Neolithic times and the Bronze Age of Shang.

In the Shang sites so far excavated the pottery finds do not compare in interest with the magnificent bronzes and jades, but one exception to this rule is a superb white pottery vessel found at the Shang capital of Anyang and now at the Freer Gallery in Washington (Plate XVII). Only two such vessels are known to exist, and their level of workmanship proves the existence of a highly developed ceramic art at this time, although, as yet, we have very scanty evidence of it. Another important find at Anyang was the discovery of shards of glazed pottery which must have been fired at some 1350 degrees centigrade which is well within the firing range of porcelain. This indicates that as early as 1400 B.C. the Chinese potters had at their disposal a technology more advanced than any in the world at that time, or for many centuries to come.

From Han times up until T'ang, that is from 206 B.C. to 618 A.D., the most interesting Chinese ceramic wares are the pottery tomb figures, known to the Chinese as *T'ao Yung*, which were buried with the dead in the belief that in the next world they would provide the deceased with all the delights which he had enjoyed in this. In Shang times some 1500 years previously it had been the custom to bury the bodies not only of humans (one royal tomb contained the decapitated heads of over a hundred persons, captives perhaps rounded up specially for this purpose), but of dogs and horses as well. But by Han times these barbarous customs had given way to the far more civilised one of burying pottery replicas of the people and the objects which the deceased would like to have with him in the next world. This has not only provided us with an invaluable glimpse into the life of this time, but with an enormous range of beautifully modelled ceramic works of art. These were not regarded at the time as works of art, but their makers were anxious to fill them with as much life and feeling as possible so that they could the better serve their masters in the next world.

The Han pieces mostly deal with the daily necessities and pleasures of this world; rather charming domestic pleasures, such as towers, pet dogs and other domestic animals, female attendants and entertainers (Plates XVIII, XIX, XX). In the warlike days of imperialist expansion of the Sui (589—618) and T'ang (618—907) the finest pieces were the war horses. Those of the Sui and earlier Six Dynasties Period (220—589) are stiff and highly stylised with enormous necks and tiny heads, and they stand rather woodenly on all four legs (in fact, four wooden peg-legs were often added to a clay body), though they possess an archaic charm all their own. But the horses of the T'ang Dynasty are by far the finest. The glazed models are usually

24

shown standing restfully at ease (Plate XXII) while the unglazed models are often shown with one foreleg pawing the earth, head bent, neck arched, and the whole body tense with barely controlled power (Plate XXIII).

During the T'ang Dynasty China became the greatest and most widespread empire in the world. Tens of thousands of foreigners came flooding into the country and brought with them a host of cultural influences: Sassanian metalwork, Graeco-Indian Buddhist sculptural forms, pottery shapes from Iran, Mesopotamia and Syria, and animal designs from the central Asian steppe-lands. Coupled with this was a spirit of self-confident energy, of hunger for new horizons and new experiences that is reflected in the vigour and variation of T'ang art. T'ang pottery is powerful and lively with sweeping sinuous curves (Plate XXV) while its decoration is often made up of flamboyant shapes and contrasting colours.

Bold new adventures in design incorporated many foreign influences and assimilated them into thoroughly Chinese forms. Advances in technology, which included the manufacture of porcelain and the discovery of many new glazes, paved the way for the Golden Age of Sung which was to follow.

The achievements of the potters of the Sung Dynasty (960—1279) were due to a happy combination of factors. The T'ang Dynasty had brought a period of unprecedented peace and prosperity, at least to central China and the south. Although by present standards the peasantry were bitterly oppressed and ill-treated, compared to the peasantry in the rest of the world at that time, even they enjoyed peace and prosperity, while the ever-increasing number of merchants, bureaucrats and landowners who lived in such cities as Hangchow had attained a degree of culture and sophistication unknown elsewhere. In the city of Chu Lu which was inundated by the Yellow River during the Sung Dynasty, there have been found pieces of porcelain which show that the everyday pots and dishes used by the citizens of that time were comparable in every way to the pieces of Tz'u Chou, Ting and Ying Ch'ing ware in the imperial collection — indeed they came from the same kilns. The presence of this vast market of prosperous and discriminating customers together with the patronage of the imperial court, provided the right conditions for the magnificent achievements of the Sung potters.

The naming of the different wares of the Sung Dynasty has been the subject of endless dispute among collectors and 'connoisseurs'. In general a term such as 'Tz'u Chou ware' has been taken to mean that a certain piece was produced in the town of Tz'u Chou in Hopei Province, while 'Chün ware' came from Chün Chou in Honan Province. But it is now known that these wares were produced at several other sites besides those named above, while at Lung Ch'üan, for instance, the traditionally recognised source of Celadon ware, wasters have been found proving that several wares were manufactured there other than that we usually call Celadon ware. It is obvious that no hard and fast scientific criteria can at present be used in dividing Sung wares into different headings. Nevertheless the labels are useful in helping us to identify groups of porcelain ware which have definite features in common.

The achievements of the Sung potters seem to illustrate a peculiar phenomenon, one might almost call it a law, of artistic development, which is that the greatest achievements in any newly discovered medium appear early on in the course of its development, while later craftsmen, although they may have a far higher level of technology at their disposal, cannot reach the same heights. This is illustrated not only in Chinese ceramic art, but even more dramatically in the bronzes which show a steady decline from Han times down to the over-elaborate excrescences of Ming and Ch'ing pieces. In sculpture there is a similar decline from the beautifully stylised Buddhist works of the northern Wei Dynasty (386—535) down to the flabby sentimentalities of later works. In Europe there are the achievements of the painters of the fifteenth and sixteenth centuries, soon after the invention of oil painting, and in photography we have the achievements of Nadar, Julia Margaret Cameron, Brady and others, working with wet-plates and hideously bulky equipment but achieving results which we have never surpassed for all our electronic flash guns.

Sung wares have only been known in Europe for some sixty years, that is since the Boxer Rebellion in 1900. Before that time it was thought that the elaborate and brightly coloured wares of the Ch'ing Dynasty (1644—1911) and late Ming (1368—1644) were the finest creations of Chinese ceramic art. The European and American *nouveaux riches* in their endless search for ostentatious bric-a-brac, turned with delight to this source of 'more than oriental splendour'. The Chinese merchants, ever eager to oblige, proceeded to supply them with Chinoiserie (or what someone has more aptly called 'Europoiserie') which consisted of great lumpy vases in garish colours, Chinese immortals in genuine *famille rose* (a term never heard of in China) and a host of other dust-catching horrors. The flood continues to this day. But in the meantime European taste has slowly been catching up with the Chinese in this matter, and now we are able to appreciate the Sung wares in all their quiet perfection of form and colour and texture. We have even learned that the later dynasties could produce pieces of exquisite workmanship, as perfect in their different way as the earlier works.

During the Ming Dynasty, and especially during the reign of the Emperor Hsuan Te (1426—36), the finest works were decorated with cobalt blue, the well-known

Blue-and-White ware. The native cobalt at first had a greyish tinge and was often supplemented with 'Mohammedan Blue' cobalt imported from the Middle East. The favourite designs consisted of writhing dragons, Buddhist emblems such as the lotus flower, or other floral designs. These early Ming bowls or stem cups were often used as altar pieces, and they have a purity of form and colour which has rarely been surpassed (Plate XXXII). During the reign of Ch'eng Hua (1465—88) coloured enamels came into general use. These consisted of ground-up coloured glass which was brushed on to the glazed porcelain and then put in an oven hot enough to melt the glass and fix it on the glaze, but not hot enough to melt the glaze itself (Plate XXXIII).

The Ch'ing Dynasty (1644—1911) is dominated by the reigns of two emperors: K'ang Hsi (1662—1723) and his grandson Ch'ien Lung (1736—96). During this span of one hundred and thirty years Chinese kilns, and especially those at the great pottery centre of Ching Te Chen, continued to produce the finest porcelain in the world. During the K'ang Hsi period the use of native cobalt in Blue-and-White ware produced a pure sapphire blue of wonderful clarity (Plate XXXV), while some of the small wine cups and stem cups have a rare delicacy and dainty 'Rococo' charm.

But after the reign of Ch'ien Lung the factories at Ching Te Chen fell on evil times, and during the nineteenth century much of the town was destroyed. The decline of the dynasty, the impoverishment of the population, and the invasion and cruel exploitation of the country as a whole led to a debasement in standards of art as well as of craftsmanship which is only now, after some hundred and fifty years, being remedied. In recent years at Tz'u Chou, Lung Ch'uan, Ching Te Chen and other historic centres, encouraging experiments are being made to restore Chinese ceramic art and industry to the level of achievement which it enjoyed in the past.

# Painting and Calligraphy

PAINTING and calligraphy have from very early times been among the accomplishments of the Chinese gentleman (the other five being listed as Ritual, Music, Archery, Charioteering and Mathematics). In no other civilisation has the ability to handle the brush been so clearly the distinguishing mark of a gentleman; a member of the privileged minority. The materials used for both writing and painting are the same, in fact the same written character is used to denote both writing and painting.

Not only has this relationship to calligraphy given painting a privileged position among the arts, in contrast to sculpture and architecture for instance, but the calligraphic qualities have tended to dominate the nature of the painting itself. For every literate Chinese has spent years in training his hand and eye in handling the paint brush and in acquiring a feeling for linear design, balance and composition. Every character is a more-or-less abstract design whose form is dictated by convention and which yet must be individually moulded by the writer to fit into the larger design of the page. Non-calligraphic elements in painting, such as modelling of form, light and shade, colour and perspective, have been relegated to second place. Painting, like calligraphy, is the language of the brush.

The earliest known form of Chinese writing dates from the Shang Dynasty (seventeenth to eleventh centuries B.C.) for the Shang people believed that while they could not speak directly to their gods and their ancestors, they could communicate with them through writing. They would scratch a message to the gods on a piece of bone or the undershell of a tortoise, then place a red hot point of bronze against the bone until it cracked, and from the direction of the cracks they would read the answering message from the gods. Thousands of fragments of these 'oracle bones' have been found at Anyang and other sites, and scholars have been able to decipher over two thousand of them.

Another form of writing from this period comes from the bronze vessels, many

*Inscriptions in a bronze vessel*

of which have incised in their surfaces the names of the ancestors whom the vessels are to honour. A few of these characters are still in pictorial form, but most are highly stylised and show a fine sense of design possessing a power and curious realism all their own. During the Warring States Period (475—221 B.C.) these characters were further conventionalised and different scripts apparently developed in the different states. One way in which this primitive stage has come down to our own day is in the form of carved stone seals which are still used to authenticate not only paintings and personal letters but business and other forms as well. The Chinese value these seals very highly both for their archaic flavour and for their subtle qualities of abstract design.

In 221 B.C. the different forms of written script were standardised, and a form much as we know it today was authorised. This was now written with the brush, and its form and construction were largely determined by the nature of the brush stroke. The variants which are now used are simply interpretations of this form. *Hsing Shu* (Running Hand) is the standard form of handwritten script, while *Ts'ao Shu* (Grass Writing) is a very free interpretation used in poems and on inscriptions where the form of the characters can be distorted almost out of all recognition so that the inscription is more like an Expressionist painting than an intellectually decipherable message. This 'Expressionism' is of course present in all Chinese calligraphy and creates that vital inner tension between the conventional form of the character as writing conveying an intellectually recognised message, and the aesthetic content of the character speak-

29

*Poem by Mi Fei (Sung Dynasty), written in* Hsing Shu *(Running Hand)*

ing the language of the emotions. It is thus that calligraphy is, in a double sense, the language of the brush.

Up until a few years ago it was thought that the hair writing and painting brush was the invention of a certain Meng T'ien in 221 B.C., but we now know that it was in common use centuries before that time, possibly as early as Shang times. In 1954

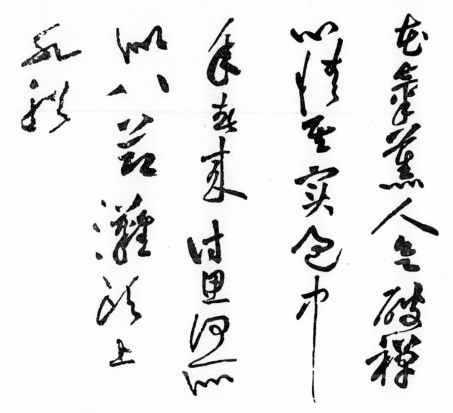

*Poem by Huang T'ing-chien, written in* Ts'ao Shu *(Grass Writing)*

a painting on silk was unearthed from a grave in Ch'angsha of the fourth century B.C. This painting was done with a brush, and already shows a high degree of skill and sophistication in the artist. The subject is a narrow-waisted elegant lady in long flowing robes shown in profile, while above her a struggle is going on between a one-legged dragon and a phoenix. Several mural paintings have been discovered in tombs of the Han Dynasty (206 B.C.—220 A.D.), and the British Museum possesses a scroll which is a very early copy of a painting by Ku K'ai-chih of the Ch'in Dynasty (265—420); but the earliest period of which we can gain any kind of a rounded picture is the T'ang (618—907).

According to the written records this was a Golden Age in painting as much as in poetry when giants like Wu Tao-tzu and Li Ssu-hsun painted incomparable master-pieces, but none of these works has survived except in the form of copies and verbal descriptions. Our greatest source of T'ang pictorial art is in the cave shrines at Tun-huang, far out on the Silk Road of the north-west. Here, between the fourth and four-teenth centuries of our era some thousand caves were hollowed out of the soft sandstone cliffs and their interiors decorated with scenes from the Buddhist scriptures. Although these paintings are the work of provincial artists, they nevertheless can give us a richly informed picture of the times both as to its everyday appearance (costume, architecture, etc.) but also its level of technical achievement. Plate XXXVI, though not by any recognised master, is a useful example of the painting of the T'ang period. Its subject matter is religious, and its style shows strong foreign influences, as in the pose and the draperies and ornaments of the god, but the powerful sweeping curves and lines, the strong bright colours and the overall sense of restless energy are typically T'ang. The female figure on the right is wearing the T'ang costume and coiffeur which were adopted by the Japanese at that time and are still worn by many Japanese women today.

During the Sung Dynasty (960—1279) Chinese painting reached full maturity. Around the imperial court at Kaifeng and later at Hangchou were gathered some of the greatest Chinese painters who ever lived. The multitude of foreign influences which had come in with the T'ang Dynasty had been thoroughly absorbed, painting and calligraphic techniques, which had been developing for two millennia, had reached an astonishing level of perfection, and a large leisured class of scholar-gentry found themselves supported and encouraged by a cultured court and a prosperous and sophisticated society. The Imperial Academy which was founded by the Emperor Hui Tsung, attracted talented artists from all over the empire. Another group of painters. was to be found among the priests of the Buddhist Ch'an Sect (Zen in Japanese) Ch'an Buddhism was eagerly accepted by these men as a synthesis of Buddhism and Taoism, leaving aside the mumbo-jumbo and flummery which had grown up around both creeds and taking from them the purity and profundity of their spiritual truths. In their paintings these priests, men such as Mu Ch'i and Liang K'ai, sought to penetrate beneath surface appearances and show the Buddha, the Divinity, that is, in all things, and through which we are united with all creation.

Many of the paintings of this period were of course nothing more than charming and pretty pictures, but the greatest of them are far more than this. The paintings by Li Ch'eng for instance (Plate XXXVIII), while it portrays a scholar's mountain retreat, an escape from the dusty world, nevertheless portrays the grandeur of nature, its rugged strength as well as its tranquility. Some of his rocks and trees could fit into a landscape by Grünewald. The Chinese accepted the harshness and cruelty of nature as part of its grandeur. In their paintings they sought to unite themselves with nature, to fit themselves into their place in the scheme of things. But their approach to this task is quite unlike that of the later European painters. A painter-scientist like Leonardo with his notebooks and anatomical sketches, or Monet with his studies of light and shade upon a haystack would be unthinkable in Sung Dynasty China. To the traditional Chinese artist such studies showed concern for the mere outward appearances, the superficial phenomena of nature, while they themselves were concerned with the inner philosophical truths which lay behind appearances.

The Ming Dynasty (1368—1644) saw a continuation of the Sung traditions, although something of the solemnity and tranquility of the Sung had gone. Already the conservative scholars were discouraging all originality and calling for a blind reverence for the past. Art critics such as Tung Ch'i-ch'ang were busy classifying all previous artists, not according to their true merits but according to their conformity to Confucian ideals.

The painters of the Sung were divided into Northern and Southern Schools, not because they had worked in the north or south, nor for any real difference in their paintings, but according to whether they had lived like true Confucian men of letters and learning (*Wen Jen*), independent of all commercial or political ties. All those who met with Tung Ch'i-ch'ang's disapproval on this score were lumped into the Northern School, while those he approved of were said to possess all the virtues of the Southern School. These classifications have been a burden to the study and appreciation of Chinese art for the last four centuries, while a more rational classification has only just begun.

One development which took place during the Ming Dynasty was the coloured woodcut. Woodcut line illustrations had been used in plays and other works of literature for centuries, but during the seventeenth century the art of making coloured woodcuts for the decoration of writing paper reached a very high level. An artist named Hu Cheng-yen, who called himself the Master of the Ten Bamboo Studio, published several collections of these coloured woodcuts. Up to this time the coloured woodcut had been considered mere handicraft, not worthy of the attention of a gentleman. But Hu was a very high official in the imperial service, and his name lent prestige to the art.

Later in the seventeenth century, another and even more famous book of woodcuts was published entitled *The Mustard Seed Garden Picture Collection*. This set out to demonstrate the different styles and techniques of the Old Masters. In beautifully drawn diagrams the author sets out the manner of drawing of everything from a blade of grass to a full landscape. By the nineteenth century this art too had declined into coarseness and vulgarity. The one branch of it which had retained much of its pristine vigour was the printing of New Year Pictures (Plate XLVII). These were printed chiefly in the towns of Yang Liu Ch'ing near Tientsin and Suchou on the Yangtze. These

33

prints were done in small primitive workshops and were sold to the peasants for a few pennies each, for them to use in decorating their cottages over the New Year holiday. While the workmanship in these peasant prints is often crude and slapdash, nevertheless they retain a fine rambunctious vigour of design and colouring, qualities which were conspicuously lacking in most of the pictorial art of the time.

By the mid-seventeenth century and with the coming of the Ch'ing Dynasty, Chinese traditional painting had almost run its course. Except for a mere handful of original masters such as Yün Shou-p'ing (Plate XLIV), who still had something new to add to the orthodox tradition of painting, the vast majority of painters were mere copyists, with nothing of their own to say. But outside the orthodox tradition there were still men of genius using the methods of Chinese painting to express their own highly individual message. Chief among these were two scions of the imperial house of Ming: Pa Ta Shan Jen, known as Chu Ta (active c. 1630–50) and Shih T'ao known as Tao Chi (active c. 1660–1710 [Plate XLV]). The painting of these two was intensely personal and expressed their anger and contempt for an 'orthodoxy' which would stoop to the service of the barbarian Manchu. Throughout the Manchu Dynasty, while the academic painting slowly withered and died, there was a succession of brave individualists who kept alive the true and living traditions of Chinese painting; men such as the monk K'un Ts'an, the Eight Eccentrics of Yang Chou, Jen Po-nien and Wu Ch'ang-shih, and in our own time, Ch'i Pai-shih. It is to these men that the young artists of modern China are turning in their study of the living traditions of Chinese painting.

# Chronological Table

| EVENTS OUTSIDE CHINA | TABLE OF DYNASTIES | MAJOR CULTURAL ACHIEVEMENTS IN CHINA |
|---|---|---|
| Egypt | **Neolithic**<br>(? — circa 18th cent. B.C.) | Painted Pottery |
| | **Shang**<br>(circa 18th cent. B.C. to circa 11th cent. B.C.) | Cast Bronze<br>Writing on Oracle Bones<br>Silk |
| Assyria<br>Greece | **Chou**<br>(circa 11th cent. B.C. to 221 B.C.)<br><br>**Ch'in**<br>(221 B.C.—206 B.C.) | Carved Jade<br>Lacquer |
| Roman Empire | **Han**<br>(206 B.C.—220 A.D.) | Proto Porcelain<br>Ordos Bronzes<br>Carved Stone Slabs |
| Dark Ages | **Six Dynasties**<br>(220—589)<br><br>**Sui**<br>(589—618) | Stone Carving in Buddhist Cave Shrines<br>Beginnings of Classical Painting |
| Charlemagne | **T'ang**<br>(618—907)<br><br>**Five Dynasties**<br>(907—960) | Porcelain<br>Pottery Tomb Figures<br>Poetry |
| Feudalism in Europe | **Sung**<br>(960—1279)<br><br>**Yuan**<br>(1279—1368) | Monochrome Porcelain<br>Painting<br><br>Drama |
| Renaissance | **Ming**<br>(1368—1644) | Polychrome Porcelain<br>Architecture |
| Industrial Revolution | **Ch'ing**<br>(1644—1911) | Decorative Arts<br>(Embroidery, Cloisonné etc.) |

# The Plates

**Plate I**  Bronze weapons. British Museum, London.
Halberd. Decorated with rams' heads. Shang Dynasty.
Axe head. Said to have been excavated at Anyang.
Spear head. Chou Dynasty.

**Plate II**  Bronze *Chüeh*. Shang Dynasty. British Museum, London.
Over twelve thousand of these ritual bronze vessels have been excavated from the tombs of the Shang and Chou Dynasties, and they have been grouped into some seventy different categories, each with a particular name, according to its shape and its presumed use. In fact, only some ten or twelve of these types are commonly found, and the four illustrated here (see also Plates III, IV, V) are among the most usual as well as the most attractive.
The exact use to which these vessels were put is uncertain, for no reliable records of the Shang rituals have come down to us, but we do know that they were used for holding the sacrificial food and wine on great occasions of state.
The remarkable shape of the *Chüeh*, and especially those two vertical knobs on the rim, has given rise to all manner of ingenious speculation. It is said to be adapted from the shape of a helmet or a stylised bird. Even sexual symbolism has been suggested. In my opinion, it is simply a spouted wine goblet with pointed feet so that it could be stood in the fire to heat the wine, and the two knobs are arrangements for lifting the heated goblet out of the fire by means of sticks placed on either side.

**Plate III**  Bronze *Chia*. Shang Dynasty, British Museum, London.

**Plate IV**  Bronze *Ku*. Cicada motif. Shang Dynasty. Mrs Marchetti Bequest, Victoria & Albert Museum, London.

**Plate V**  Bronze *Tsun* in the shape of an owl. Shang Dynasty. Victoria & Albert Museum, London.

**Plate VI**  Bronze buckle in the form of a leaping tiger. Han Dynasty. British Museum, London.

**Plate VII**  Bronze figures of deer from north China. 'Ordos bronze' style. Probably Han Dynasty. British Museum, London. *Notes continued on page 85*

36

III

IX A

IX B

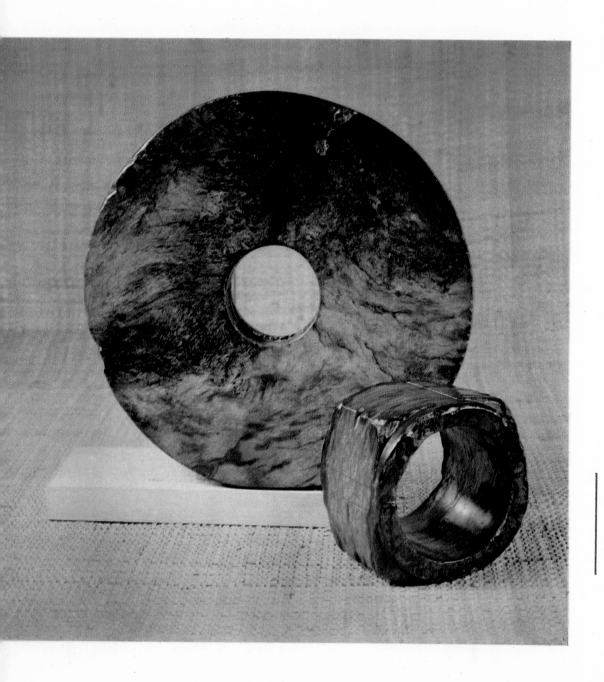

X

XI

XII

XIII

XIV

XV

XXI

XXIII

XXVII

XXXIII

引路菩

XXXVI

XXXVIII

XXXIX

XL

XLI

XLII

XLIII

XLIV

XLVII

XLVIII

In the Ordos grasslands enclosed by the great northward loop of the Yellow River, many hundreds of these small bronze figures have been found. Other similar figures have been found on different sites all across the Eurasian land mass. They are quite different in style from the conventionalised monsters on the Shang bronzes. They are intensely lifelike, obviously modelled by artists who were fully familiar with their subjects. Their use is uncertain; perhaps they were simply ornaments, but it is more likely that they were some form of amulet looked to for their symbolism of fertility, or some form of symphathetic magic, to give luck in hunting.

During the T'ang Dynasty the Chinese were brought into close contact with the civilisations of India, the Middle East and central Asia, and their art forms were influenced and greatly enriched by these contacts. From the Sassanid empire, in what is now Persia, came a form of finely wrought metalwork which made use of delicately incised designs of flowers, animals and curving lines. These silver pieces are good examples of the Chinese adaption of the Sassanian style.

The round *Pi* of green jade is said to have represented Heaven, while the hollow square *Ts'ung* represented the earth.

Some time in the Six Dynasties period the first Buddha images were brought from India to China, and in the cave shrines of Lung Men, Yun Kang and Mai Chi Shan tens of thousands of these images were carved out of the native stone or modelled in clay (see also Plate XIII). During the early centuries, these figures showed a skilful blending of Indian mysticism, Greek classical beauty and Chinese harmony and moderation. But after the tenth century they tended to become rather flabby and empty.

A Bodhisattva is a saintly being who has attained enlightenment, but has delayed his entry into Paradise in order to help others along the way.

Fine African ivory was brought to China by the Arabs as early as the T'ang Dynasty. By the seventeenth century the Chinese themselves were sailing to the east coast of Africa and bringing back vast quantities of ivory.

**Plate XVI**  Neolithic painted pot from Kansu. British Museum, London.
This fine buff-coloured earthenware was constructed by the use of the 'Coil Method'. The sweeping curves and geometric designs are typical of this style.

**Plate XVII**  White pottery jar of the Late Shang Dynasty. The Smithsonian Institution, Freer Gallery of Art, Washington, D.C.
Hard white unglazed clay with carved design. Only two such white pottery jars are known to exist complete.

**Plate XVIII**  Pottery watchdog with iridescent glaze. Grave figure from the Han Dynasty. British Museum, London.
In China in the second millennium B.C. the burial of a king would be accompanied by the sacrifice of scores of slaves, as well as of horses and dogs. By the time of the Han Dynasty the objects buried were simply clay models of whatever the deceased might require for an enjoyable life in the next world. These were often such things as those illustrated in Plates XIX and XX, which display a rather charming delight in simple pleasures.

**Plate XIX**  Pottery pleasure pavilion. Grave object. Han Dynasty. British Museum, London.

**Plate XX**  Bull in pigmented pottery. Grave figure. Six Dynasties. British Museum, London.

**Plate XXI**  Earth spirit. Grave figure. T'ang Dynasty. British Museum, London.
By the time of the T'ang Dynasty, these grave figures had become more dramatic and exotic: demonic earth spirits, bellowing camels and, above all, magnificent war-horses (see Plates XXII and XXIII).

**Plate XXII**  Horse in glazed pottery. Grave figure. T'ang Dynasty. British Museum, London.

**Plate XXIII**  Horse in unglazed pottery, with traces of pigment. T'ang Dynasty. Museum of Eastern Art, Oxford.

**Plate XXIV**  Figures in glazed pottery. T'ang Dynasty. British Museum, London.

**Plate XXV**  Bird-headed pottery ewer. T'ang Dynasty. British Museum, London.

**Plate XXVI**  Ying Ch'ing ware. Sung Dynasty. British Museum, London.
*Ying Ch'ing* means shadow blue-green. Both the form and the colour of these pieces are very subtle, the colour showing most clearly where the glaze has pooled in the hollows.

**Plate XXVII**  Kuan ware. Sung Dynasty. British Museum, London.
*Kuan* means official, and these pieces were specially made for the imperial court. The 'crackle' was produced by skilfully controlling the firing.

**Plate XXVIII**    Ting ware. Sung Dynasty. British Museum, London.

This ware was produced at Ting Chou in Hopei Province.

**Plate XXIX**    Tz'u Chou ware. Sung and Ming Dynasties. British Museum, London.

The white body of this stoneware is covered with a white or black slip, and on this the decoration is painted or incised. In some cases this would again be covered by a coloured glaze. This is the only Sung ware in which the design is painted under the glaze.

**Plate XXX**    Celadon ware. Sung Dynasty. Percival David Foundation, London.

This ware has a grey porcellaneous body. It is especially noted for the fineness of the designs which are incised under the glaze.

**Plate XXXI**    Chün ware. Sung Dynasty. Percival David Foundation, London.

This ware sometimes appears with violent purple splashes, but the finest pieces are those, such as this oviform jar, in which the glaze is a milky opalescent blue with only a hint of purple.

**Plate XXXII**    Plate and stem cup. Hsüan Te period (1426—35). Percival David Foundation, London.

The blue here is deep but not brilliant, and was obtained from the cobalt pigment known as 'Mohammedan blue', imported from the Near East.

**Plate XXXIII**    Cups and stem cup. Ch'eng Hua period (1465—87). Percival David Foundation, London.

The stem cup and the lower wine cup are from the Ch'eng Hua period — the classical period for coloured enamels. The upper wine cup is of the same design but of the much later K'ang Hsi period (1662—1722).

**Plate XXXIV**    Wine cups. K'ang Hsi period (1662—1722). British Museum, London.

The fine translucent porcelain and clear coloured enamels are typical of the best K'ang Hsi ware.

**Plate XXXV**    Jar. K'ang Hsi period (1662—1722). British Museum, London.

'Hawthorn pattern', blue and white. Chinese cobalt had by this time been refined to the purest sapphire blue.

**Plate XXXVI**    *Kuan Yin guiding a soul*. T'ang Dynasty. British Museum, London.

This painting was found at Tunhuang, and is probably a tenth-century copy of an earlier T'ang original. Kuan Yin originated in India as a male god named Avolo-kitesvara, and early pictures such as this one show the god wearing a moustache; but in the course of time the Chinese came to think of Kuan Yin as a goddess. On the left are depicted the Mansions of Paradise.

**Plate XXXVII**    *Streams and mountains without end*. Anonymous painter of the Sung Dynasty. Cleveland Museum of Art, Ohio.

This is a detail taken from a long handscroll.

**Plate XXXVIII** *A temple on a clear day in the mountains*, by Li Ch'eng (active 960—90). Hanging scroll. The Nelson Gallery, Atkins Museum, Kansas City, Missouri.

**Plate XXXIX** *Landscape*, by Yen Tz'u-yü (twelfth-thirteenth cent.). Album leaf. The Smithsonian Institution, Freer Gallery of Art, Washington, D.C.

**Plate XL** *Bamboo*, attributed to Wu Chen (1280—1354). Album leaf. British Museum, London. This is an impressive example of a painting which is both realistic and abstract — both a painting and a work of calligraphy. Each part of the bamboo is completed in a single calligraphic brushstroke. Even the dry-brush effect is used to lend liveliness to the contours of the leaves. The energy and superbly controlled power of the brushwork convey a direct impression of the life-force within the growing bamboo. This is the double language of the brush — the descriptive and the emotive.

**Plate XLI** *Bird on a branch*, attributed to Emperor Hui Tsung (1082—1135). Album leaf. British Museum, London.

**Plate XLII** *The Emperor Kuang Wu fording a river*, by Ch'iu Ying (1620—91). National Gallery of Canada, Ottawa.

**Plate XLIII** *River landscape*, by Chu Tuan. Dated 1501. Ostasiatiska Museet, Stockholm. Painted in the style of Kuo Hsi. Chu Tuan was a follower of the northern Sung academic tradition.

**Plate XLIV** *Flowers*, by Yün Shou-p'ing (1633—90). Hanging scroll. British Museum, London. This is a good example of Yün Shou-p'ing's use of transparent washes of soft colour.

**Plate XLV** *Landscape*, by Shih T'ao (active 1660—1710). Album leaf. Museum für Ostasiatische Kunst, Cologne.

**Plate XLVI** *Bird and blossoms*. Woodcut from the Ten Bamboo Studio (1644). British Museum, London. Hu Cheng-yen, the Master of the Ten Bamboo Studio, was regarded as the greatest of the Chinese woodcut artists. His *Pictures from the Ten Bamboo Studio* is the most famous collection of its kind.

**Plate XLVII** *Door god*. Peasant New Year picture from Soochow (nineteenth century). Author's Collection. Such pictures were bought by the peasants at the New Year festival to decorate their homes.

**Plate XLVIII** *Landscape*, by Fu Pao-shih. British Museum, London. Fu Pao-shih is a contemporary painter, a professor at the Nanking Institute of Education. He draws on traditional sources, especially the painters of the. Sung Dynasty, but his style and subject matter are modern.

## DATE DUE